Henry Darling

Slavery and the War

A historical essay

Henry Darling

Slavery and the War
A historical essay

ISBN/EAN: 9783744731300

Printed in Europe, USA, Canada, Australia, Japan

Cover: Foto ©ninafisch / pixelio.de

More available books at **www.hansebooks.com**

Slavery and the War:

A Historical Essay.

BY

REV. HENRY DARLING, D.D.

" Love thou thy land, with love far brought
From out the storied Past, and used
Within the Present, but transfused
Through future time, by power of thought."—TENNYSON.

PHILADELPHIA:

J. B. LIPPINCOTT & CO.

1863.

SLAVERY AND THE WAR.

From the commencement of that internecine war, which is now raging with so much fury in our country, the faith that it would eventuate in the entire destruction of American slavery was, with many good men, strong. They had long stood appalled before this gigantic national evil, afraid almost to utter in words the sentiments of condemnation that were burning in their hearts, and entirely unable to see how any exodus was to be opened for the enslaved. The problem was too profound for human solution. Girt around with constitutional defenses, and its righteousness maintained by the teachings of almost every pulpit in the South, an institution, once universally confessed to be but temporary, and destined before the march of civilization and religion to pass away, seemed fast imbedding itself indissolubly, into the very structure of a large part of American society.

But how changed was the whole aspect of this question, the very moment that this great national sin, in its vaulting ambition, grappled with liberty, and sought to hurl into the dust, the very institutions that had fostered its greatness! Timid philanthropists and religionists then saw, at once, that God had taken this problem, so insoluble with them, into His hands, and that now again, in the eyes of all the nations, would that prophecy of Christ be fulfilled— "All they that take the sword shall perish with the sword."

Doubtless at the outset, this expectation of the final issue was, as to the mode of its accomplishment, vague. Men walked to this sublime conclusion by a simple faith. Unable to believe that the purpose of God in permitting this rebellion was our national ruin, but seeing in it His design to cleanse and purify us, in what other direction could the process extend but in this? True, slavery was not our only national sin. We had other evils over which to mourn, and to rid us of which, we well deserved the judgments of

(3)

God. But all these, individually considered or aggregated, what were they when once compared with the single fact of the enslavement of nearly four millions of people? Are other demons to be exorcised from our body politic, and this one to remain? Is God bringing us through this terrible baptism of blood, to cleanse the white robe of our national purity from a few of its minor impurities, but yet to permit this deepest, darkest stain to remain? That would be a strange teleology, indeed, that would lead any to such a conclusion.

And this faith in the ultimate issue of our struggle, cherished by many, the very moment that hostilities were commenced, how wonderfully has every subsequent event confirmed it! God has given us, in this rebellion, what we have been wont to call *dark days*, but in reality they were bright ones. He has suffered our armies sometimes to be defeated; but our greatest *moral* victories have been at those very seasons achieved. What if it had been otherwise? What, if over the defenses of Manassas, or through the swamps of the Chickahominy, or across the Rappahannock and the Rapidan, our armies had marched to victory? Would not the *Union*, in all probability, have been restored upon its old basis, and slavery have gone on for many centuries to come, sustained in its present possessions, if not extended by all the defenses of the Federal Constitution? It is nothing but these very defeats which have rendered such a supposition improbable, if not impossible. But for them Congress might never have passed the Confiscation Act, nor the President have issued his proclamation of emancipation to the enslaved. It was the successes of the rebellion that *constrained* this legislation. They were dernier resorts, extra-constitutional acts — it may be — adopted by our civil authorities reluctantly, and only from the necessities of self-preservation.

And thus has it been all along in the history of this struggle. We often marvel at the hot haste with which some European powers acknowledged these rebels against our Government as "*belligerents*"; and we can hardly repress the indignation that we feel against our mother country, for the substantial sympathy she has given them. Previous to the outbreak of this war, no one could for a moment have imagined, that England would have pursued such a policy toward us, as she has. But recently, herself, delivered from a fearful rebellion which threatened to tear from her one of her largest possessions, and to quell which she had to pour out not a little of her most precious blood, we were all ready to expect her warmest sympathy with us in a similar peril. But may we not, in the issue to which it must lead, felicitate ourselves that she has denied us this?—ay! that she has given that very sympathy which we had anticipated for ourselves, to our enemies? Had it been as we hoped, the sword would, long ere this, have been sheathed. It has been foreign sympathy and aid, together with the hope of foreign intervention and recognition, that has made the leaders of this rebellion so persistent in their treason. They have not desisted in their mad purpose, because voices of hope have ever been coming to them from beyond the sea.

But did many good men, at the commencement of this war, by *faith*, see in its final issue the destruction of American slavery? Did they believe that its *mission* was to us, as was that of Moses to Pharaoh, and that we should finally behold a second exodus of the enslaved? It is now more than faith which apprehends such a result. We can almost walk by *sight* to this sublime conclusion.

One of the profoundest thinkers of our age, in speaking of the relations that this war sustains to American slavery, remarks: "I cannot see how any Southern man, desiring that slavery should be continued and perpetuated, can be willing to permit this war to be a long one; nor can I see how any Northern man, hoping and praying for the destruction of slavery, can desire that the war should be a short one." The argument is well put, and no candid mind, we think, can fail to admit its truthfulness Liberty must follow in the wake of our invading armies. The gradual disintegration of domestic servitude, is one of the natural processes of a war like this. Slavery must flee before our advancing hosts, as darkness flies before the light. Many slaves voluntarily come into the Federal lines, others fall into those lines from necessity, and few of either class can ever be made again to wear the yoke of bondage. Some are brought under the advantages of a partial education, a few are armed, all taste of the sweets of personal liberty, and are thus unfitted, by a threefold influence, for future servitude. At every point, in the domain of slavery, where our arms have already established themselves, the process of emancipation is actually going on. A flag of freedom is unfurled, and under its folds, in rapidly augmenting numbers, are gathered the enslaved. It has been estimated, that in this way, more than one hundred and fifty thousand slaves, have already been made freemen.

Moreover, where these influences have not as yet been felt, where the rebellion is still in full power, the necessities of war have required the resort, on the part of our enemies, to an expedient that is itself full of peril to the stability of slavery. A very large number of slaves, withdrawn from their labor on isolated plantations, and in quiet villages, have been congregated in cities, or at other points of peril, to build forts, or to dig trenches, or in some other way to aid in the defenses of their masters. Will these, when again remanded to their quiet home-labor, be the same peaceful and willing subjects of oppression that they once were ? Is it possible to conceive that, while thus employed, some true conception of the nature of this struggle will not find its way into even their besotted intellect, so that, ever after, the North Star will shine more brightly to their vision, and be more attractive to their fugitive feet ?

And these natural processes of the war, eliminating slavery, must only increase as it continues to be vigorously waged. The more the wedge is driven, the broader will be the rent, and the deeper down will it run. Old centers of light brightening, will throw out their beams farther into the darkness; and new ones kindled will scatter a darkness that still remains unbroken. Along the Atlantic seaboard and the Gulf of Mexico, from the mouth of the Delaware to the Rio Grande, there was not, a twelvemonth ago, a single point where freedom had a home. That whole line of sea-coast, with a vast territory stretching away to the north and west, was in the undisputed possession of slavery. As, however, by the prowess of our arms, forts, navy-yards, and cities have all along that coast been wrested from rebel hands, they have each one become—unintentionally, perhaps, but from very necessity—free homes for the enslaved. Events have daily occurred there that were never known before. Labor has been remunerated, ignorance instructed, and bondmen made free. And shall this process continue for another twelvemonth ? Shall these *free homes* for the enslaved not only go on with their great work of emancipation, but be multiplied all along that coast ? Shall Wilmington, Charleston, and Mobile be added to Norfolk, Beaufort, and New Orleans ? How could slavery survive the potency of such influences, working—at *her very heart*—her destruction ?

But further, how disastrous, in its results to slavery, must be the simple continuance by our navy of the present blockade of the Southern ports ! Perhaps no country in the world ever enjoyed so complete a monopoly of a great staple of trade as the States now in rebellion against this government. The cotton manufactories of England and France, supposed to give employment to more than a million and a half of persons, and to yield an annual income in England alone of thirty-six millions pounds sterling, have for the last twenty-five years, received from these States, more than four-fifths of their supplies.* At the commencement of this century the amount of cotton grown in this country was inconsiderable. The United States then yielded but a small fraction of the aggregate production of the world. But ever since that, the quantity grown here has been rapidly increasing, while that produced elsewhere—India and Egypt excepted—has materially lessened. By an official report made to the Congress of the United States in the year 1835, it appears that while the total production of raw cotton for the previous year (1834) was 900,000,000 pounds, 460,000,000 pounds were exported from our own land.† And it is the growth of this trade, rapid beyond all commercial precedent, that has enriched these States, made slavery to them a profitable institution, and given them, in this struggle, to so great a degree the sympathy of foreign nations. Indeed, the monopoly of this great staple has been the bulwark of American slavery. It was this that arrested that process of emancipation, which had before been gradually extending itself as a great tide of blessing over our whole land, and which wrought—as we shall hereafter more fully see—a great revolution of sentiment, even at the South, in regard to the moral character of this institution. There is much truth in that adage, regarded commercially, " Cotton is King."

· But already does the throne of this monarch totter. Already, has the monopoly of this article, possessed so long by the Southern States, been hopelessly broken. Should peace be restored to-day, the commercial world will never be *as dependent* upon this country, for her supply of cotton, as she has been. Other sources have been opened for this supply, and through them will no inconsiderable portion, of the raw material, be hereafter procured. The blockade of the Southern ports of this country, preventing the exportation of cotton, has already greatly stimulated its growth, in every other land, adapted by climate and soil for its production. And let this condition of things exist much longer, let the supply of cotton from this country to England and France be cut off for

---

* Penny Cyclopædia, article *Cotton.*
† See Woodbury's Report to the House of Representatives.

another twelvemonth, and what though then her ports be opened to the commerce of the world, other nations will have wrested forever from her grasp this great scepter of power. India, Egypt, and South Africa will then supply the looms of Manchester, Stockport, and Glasgow. Fields heretofore sown in cotton, will be planted in wheat, or corn. Slavery will cease to be an economical institution; and conscience, no longer perverted by the profits of unrequited labor, will instinctively speak out its abhorrence of human servitude.

Nor can we see that the issue would be materially changed, should we allow the supposition of a failure of our arms, and the consequent establishment, as a separate nation, of the States now in rebellion against this government. Admitting, for argument sake, such a result of this struggle, and could the slavery of the black race long remain as an institution of the new Confederacy? Its geographical boundary to the North, wherever drawn, could be but imaginary. With no great rivers or mountains flowing across our continent, a line of separation between the new government, and the old Union, could exist only on parchment. For fifteen hundred miles, and more, slavery and freedom would lie side by side; no physical barriers would separate them. Could darkness bear such proximity to light?

We should remember that, upon the supposition now made, it is highly probable, if not certain, that there would be everywhere in the old Union the most intense aversion to slavery. Its citizens would rightfully regard it as the cause of all their national troubles, and, instead of apologizing for it, and looking kindly upon it, as many now do, all would denounce and execrate it. Any provision for the rendition of fugitive slaves would then be impossible. Every bondman would be free the very moment that, crossing that imaginary line of demarkation between the two nations, his feet should tread upon our soil. Ay, more! to cross that line he would be invited, if not by actual legislation, yet by the warm sympathies of our whole people. Surely "the spider's most attenuated web, were cord and cable," to the feeble hold that the slaveholder would then have upon his human chattel. An early morning walk, a quiet stroll at evening, the leaping of a fence, the fording of a little stream, a certain road to liberty, who among the enslaved would not walk in it? Freedom, when brought into such a contact with slavery, would encroach very rapidly upon her domain. She would extend her lines farther and farther into the dominion of her enemy; nor could the process be well impeded until her whole territory should thus be gradually, but surely, wrested from her grasp.

Moreover, looking at the physical and social condition of the States that would thus be confederated, do we not see that many of them contain in themselves elements, that could not long be quiet and submissive, in a government built upon slavery as its corner-stone?

A single glance at the map of this country will show almost every Slave State to be divided into two sections, differing very widely from each other in their physical geography. One is hilly and rugged, and is formed by those two mountain ranges which, running in almost parallel lines through the center of Virginia, and from thence through Western North Carolina, and Eastern Tennessee, terminate in Northern Georgia, and Alabama. The other is level and low, and stretches northward, and westward, from the Atlantic, and the Gulf. And as these two sections contrast in their physical aspect, so do they in climate, productions, structure of society, political views, and necessities. One is adapted to the growth of the great staples of a semi-tropical climate; in the other the cereal grains of the North are most cultivated. In one section, the people—save in the large cities—are almost wholly engaged in agricultural pursuits; in the other, the facilities for manufactories invite their establishment. The one is peopled by large landholders, of high, social, and sometimes intellectual culture, but of a proud and arrogant spirit; the other by a comparatively rude and simple people, of limited possessions. The one, in its political policy, favors free trade; the other has its interest best subserved by some protection to home industry. In the one slavery seems almost indigenous, has grown into gigantic proportions, and is doubtless pecuniarily profitable; in the other it is an exotic, has never so firmly interwoven itself into the structure of society, and is perhaps pecuniarily a burden. And now can it be supposed that this latter section, this mountain region, this land along whose streams are slowly springing up manufacturing establishments, this land of hardy industry and small farms, would long submit to a government, that is wholly in the interest of the rich aristocratic cotton-growers of the low country, and that has been established entirely for their aggrandizement? Already has that part of this great section of the South, which borders upon freedom, asserted that it had no sympathy with this new Confederacy.

Western Virginia is, upon any supposition that we can make as to the issue of this war, indissolubly connected with the North; and so, doubtless, would Eastern Tennessee be, could she but have had her own election in the matter. And the other portions of this same section, though for a little season drawn into such an alliance, could not in it be long retained. There is not, in a word, at the South itself, we contend, that homogeneousness which is essential to a slave oligarchy. Such a government would contain in itself, the seeds, of its own dissolution.

We have no hesitation, then, in affirming, as our settled conviction, that the issue of this war will be the entire destruction of American slavery. Each fact in the unfolding of this bloody tragedy, has only helped us on to this conclusion. We walked by faith, timidly but hopefully, to this result when the first clash of arms broke upon our astonished ear, but now we walk to it by sight, boldly, and without any fear of disappointment. True, we may be slow in reaching this sublime goal. Great social evils do not ordinarily either come or go, as did Jonah's gourd, in a night. There may yet be many a convulsive throe of this hydra before it dies. But the death-blow has been given it, and all the political revolutions that are now shaking our land, are but its dying agonies.

With this deep conviction, we propose in this article, not indeed to write the *obituary* of slavery, but to seek to rescue from oblivion, some great facts in its history, that may afford the material for those who will hereafter be called to perform this office.

We will first briefly glance at the history of slavery during our colonial dependence, show how generally the colonists regarded the system as unrighteous, and how stoutly they all resisted its extension in their midst.

Every one, at all familiar with the early history of this country, is aware of the way in which slavery was here introduced. In the month of August, 1620—a little more than thirteen years after the first permanent English settlement was made on this continent, and four months before the Puritan colony landed at Plymouth—a Dutch man-of-war entered the James River, and sold to the colonists twenty Guinea negroes. The additions, however, that for the next few years were made to this number, must have been quite inconsiderable, for in 1650 we find that the proportion of slaves to freemen in the colony was but one to fifty. It was not until

James II., in 1672, chartered a company, for the express purpose of trading in slaves, under the name of "The Royal African Company," that the institution of slavery may be said to have become established in the Virginia colony.

But all this transpired, let it be here carefully noted, unsanctioned by any colonial legislation. The system domesticated itself in the colony gradually and surreptitiously; and while the immediate demand for laborers in a new country, doubtless blinded the eyes of the colonists to the evils that domestic servitude would ultimately entail upon them, yet never did it lead them in any way to give to this institution the least legal sanction. Indeed "there is not," says Bancroft, "in all the colonial legislation of America, *one single law which recognizes the rightfulness of slavery in the abstract.*"* The colony at first passed by the subject in silence. Too weak to utter any protest against it, it passively suffered its introduction. But this silence was soon broken; and the first slave-holding colony in this country, by a long series of legislative enactments, uttered, in no uncertain words, her severe condemnation of that very system, to conserve and perpetuate which, she is now seeking to destroy our National Government.

But, before noticing the strenuous opposition that the Virginia colony made, to the extension of slavery in its midst, there is one fact, common to all the colonies, which, as it strikingly illustrates how general was then the belief that Christianity was opposed to slavery, we will do well here to mention. From New England to Carolina, the opinion that, by consenting to the baptism of his slave, the master virtually enfranchised him, was almost universal. The colonists did not believe that a man could become the Lord's freeman, and yet remain in bondage to his fellow-man. And how deep and general this sentiment was, we may judge from the fact that the three colonial legislatures of Maryland, Virginia, and South Carolina, gave a negative to it by special enactments. As an example, we quote a brief section from the act passed by the legislature of Maryland in 1715:—

"Forasmuch as many people have neglected to baptize their negroes, or suffer them to be baptized, on a vain apprehension that negroes, by receiving the sacrament of baptism are manumitted and set free—Be it enacted, etc., That no negro or negroes, by receiving the holy sacrament of baptism, is thereby manumitted or set free, nor hath any right or title

* Vol. iii. p. 409.

to freedom or manumission more than he had before, any law, usage, or custom to the contrary notwithstanding."*

The crown lawyers of England, also, declared this sentiment of the colonists to be erroneous. Yorke and Talbot, his Majesty's Attorney and Solicitor-General, pronounced it lawful to retain a baptized negro in slavery; and these opinions were printed, and widely circulated in the colonies. And to this same end was likewise the power of the Church evoked. Gibson, the Bishop of London, declared that "Christianity and the embracing of the Gospel does not make the least alteration in civil property."†

In a case, tried before the Judges of the King's Bench in England, in 1696, and where the question, whether the baptism of a negro slave, *without* the privity or consent of his master, emancipated him? underwent an elaborate discussion, the counsel for the slave thus presented the moral argument upon the affirmative:—

"Being baptized according to the use of the Church, he (the slave) is thereby made a Christian; * * but if the duties which arise from such a condition cannot be performed in a state of servitude, the baptism must be manumission. That such duties cannot be performed is plain; for the persons baptized are to be confirmed by the Diocesan, when they give an account of their faith, and are enjoined by several acts of Parliament to come to church. But if the master hath an absolute property over him, then he might send him far enough from the performance of those duties, viz., into Turkey, or any other country of infidels, where they neither can or will be suffered to exercise the Christian religion. * * It is observed among the Turks that they do not make slaves of those of their own religion, though taken in war; and if a Christian be so taken, yet if he renounce Christianity and turn Mohammedan, he doth thereby obtain his freedom. And if this be a custom allowed among infidels, then baptism, in a Christian nation, as this is, should be an immediate enfranchisement to them, as they should thereby acquire the privileges and immunities enjoyed by those of the same religion, and be entitled to the laws of England."‡

But to return to the history of the Virginia colony. Slavery, introduced silently, and without any legal sanction among this people, was afterward, as we have affirmed, stoutly resisted in its extension, by a long course of legislative enactments. Let us instance a few of these.

<hr>

* Act of 1715, ch. xliv. sec. 23.
† Bancroft, vol. iii. p. 409.
‡ Stroud's Laws of Slavery, p. 67.

At a very early period, some time prior to 1662—but forty years, let it be observed, after the introduction of slavery into Virginia—its increase in the colony was sought to be checked by the imposition of a tax upon *female* slaves.* At first this tax was only five per cent., and, to avoid the jealousy of English traders, was made payable by the buyer; but as this did not accomplish the desired end, the duty was from time to time increased, until at last it amounted to four times that sum. All discrimination, likewise, of sex was finally removed. Every negro imported into the colony was subject to an impost of twenty per cent.; and though from this high duty, amounting almost to a prohibition, there was subsequently a considerable decline, yet this mode of checking, if not entirely destroying, the importation of slaves by the imposition of a tax, was never wholly abandoned, until the royal veto forbade its continuance.† In 1726, Hugh Drysdale, the Deputy-Governor of Virginia, announced to the House of Burgesses that the "*interfering interest* of the *African Company*"—a company chartered by the English government, and who enjoyed the monopoly of the slave-trade—had obtained the repeal of all laws imposing any tax upon the importation of slaves into that colony.‡

But though these praiseworthy efforts to restrain the slave-trade, and ultimately to exclude slavery from the colony, continued for a long series of years, were thus brought to a violent and disastrous end, by the interference of the British crown, yet "a deeply-seated public opinion began more and more to avow the evils and the injustice of slavery itself;" and in 1761 it was proposed to suppress the importation of Africans by a prohibitory duty:—

"Among those," says Bancroft, "who took part in the long and violent debate," which this motion occasioned, "was Richard Henry Lee. * * In the continued importation of slaves, he foreboded danger to the political and moral interests of the Old Dominion; an increase of the free Anglo-Saxons, he argued, would foster arts and varied agriculture, while a race doomed to abject bondage was of necessity an enemy to social happiness. He painted from ancient history the horrors of servile insurrections. He deprecated the barbarous atrocity of the trade with Africa, and its violation of the equal rights of men created like ourselves in the image of God. 'Christianity,' thus he spoke in conclusion, 'by introducing into Europe the truest principles of universal benevo-

* Bancroft, vol. i. p. 173.
† Tucker's Blackstone, vol. ii., Appendix, p. 49.
‡ Bancroft, vol. iii. p. 415.

lence and brotherly love, happily abolished slavery. Let us who profess
the same religion practice its precepts, and by agreeing to this duty pay
a proper regard to our true interests, and to the dictates of justice and
humanity.'"*

The motion prevailed. The prohibitory tax was imposed. The
colonial legislature, did everything it was competent to do, to banish this evil from the colony. It was thoroughly awake to the
enormities of the system; but the statute was immediately vetoed
by the English crown.

But every effort to banish slavery, by the imposition of a heavy
tax upon imported slaves, thus defeated, the Virginia Assembly
resorted to a new expedient. In 1772, they petitioned the King
upon this subject, and how remarkable was their language ! It
must savor not a little of fanaticism for many modern conservatives
to read such stirring words. Indeed, with what is now trans-
piring in the Old Dominion, there is nothing short of the verity
of history, that could make us believe that such a document ever
emanated from such a source :—

"We are encouraged." say they, "to look up to the throne and implore your Majesty's paternal assistance in averting a calamity of a most
alarming nature. The importation of slaves into the colonies from the
coast of Africa hath long been considered as a trade of great inhumanity,
and under its present encouragement, we have too much reason to fear,
will *endanger the existence of your Majesty's* American dominions. We
are sensible that some of your Majesty's subjects in Great Britain may
reap emolument from this sort of traffic ; but when we consider that it
greatly retards the settlement of the colonies with useful inhabitants,
and may in time have the most destructive influence, we presume to hope
that the interest of a few will be disregarded, when placed in competition
with the security and happiness of such numbers of your Majesty's dutiful
and loyal subjects.

"Deeply impressed with these sentiments, we most humbly beseech
your Majesty to remove all those restraints on your Majesty's governors
of this colony which inhibit their assenting to such laws as might check
so very pernicious a commerce."†

And that this petition might receive the favorable regard of the
British ministry, some of those distinguished philanthropists in
England, who were then pleading so eloquently the cause of the
enslaved, were informally solicited personally to press its reception

---

* Bancroft, vol. iv. p. 422.
† Princeton Repertory, vol. xxxiv. p. 536.

upon the crown. And to this request they cheerfully complied. Granville Sharpe, who had just immortalized himself by the defense of the poor negro, Somerset, and who, in that memorable case, had secured a decision which not only cleared Somerset, but determined that slavery could not exist in Great Britain, waited personally on the Secretary of State, and urged the righteousness of the petition.* But it was all in vain. The policy of England with regard to slavery in the American colonies was fixed. She would not suffer it to pollute her own soil; but at the same time she would force its acceptance, and extension, upon her citizens abroad. And doubtless unwilling, by the direct refusal of so righteous a request, to manifest to the world her true purpose, she added to her virtual rejection of this petition, the indignity of profound silence. No reply was ever made to this request of the colony, and slavery, under the ægis of the British crown, went on, fastened herself more and more deeply, into the structure of American society.

But as exhibiting still further the opposition of the Virginia colony to the institution of African slavery—an opposition that but for the interference of Great Britain would have certainly issued in its destruction—we should add to these legislative enactments, the utterances of some of her most distinguished sons, and the incidental references to this fact that may be found, in some of her official documents. Madison says :—

"The *British government constantly* checked the attempts of Virginia to put *a stop to this infernal traffic.*"†

In the preamble to the Constitution of that State, promulgated n the 29th of June, 1776, we read :—

"Whereas, George III., King, etc., heretofore intrusted with the exercise of the kingly office in this government, hath endeavored to pervert the same into a detestable and insupportable tyranny, by prompting our negroes to rise in arms among us—*those very negroes whom, by an inhuman use of the negative, he hath refused us permission to exclude by law*—Therefore Resolved," etc.‡

And it was doubtless the memory of the same facts, present to the mind of Jefferson, another of Virginia's illustrious sons, that

---

* Tucker's Blackstone, vol. ii., Appendix, pp. 51 and 52.
† Madison Papers, 3, 1390.
‡ Stroud's Laws of Slavery, p. 37.

led him, in the original draft of the Declaration of Independence, to instance, as one of the reasons for separating ourselves from the government of George III., the fact that—"Determined to keep open a market where men *should be bought and sold, he had prostituted his negative for suppressing every legislative attempt to prohibit or restrain this execrable commerce*," a clause which was erased by Congress, not because it deviated from historic truth, or failed to express the sentiments of a large majority of its members, but, as Jefferson himself said, because "the pusillanimous idea that we had friends in England worth keeping terms with, still haunted the minds of many."[*]

And what we have thus endeavored to show was true of Virginia, was measurably true of all the other English continental colonies. "In the aggregate," says Bancroft, "they were always opposed to the African slave-trade," * * and laws designed to restrict importations of slaves are scattered copiously along the records of colonial legislation.[†] Should there be any exception to this remark, many circumstances would point us at once to South Carolina. Of the original thirteen States of this Union, she *alone* was from the cradle, essentially a planting State, with slave labor. The institution of involuntary servitude is coeval with the first plantations on Ashley River. It was likewise observed from the first, that the climate of South Carolina was more congenial to the African than that of the more northern colonies, and hence she early became the principal point to which slavers brought their human chattels. Indeed, so rapid was the importation of Africans into this colony, that in a few years they were to the whites in the proportion of twenty-two to twelve, a proportion that had no parallel north of the West Indies.[‡] The German traveler, Von Reck, in 1734 reported the number of negroes in South Carolina as 30,000, and for the annual importation gave the exaggerated estimate of 3000.[§]

But this rapid increase of bondmen did not take place, *even in South Carolina*, without exciting alarm, and without the attempt being at least twice made by its legislature to check this evil, if not entirely remove it. In 1715 a duty of ten pounds was imposed

---

[*] Elliot's Debates on the Federal Constitution, vol. i. p. 60.
[†] Bancroft, vol. iii. pp. 410 and 411.
[‡] Ibid., vol ii. p. 171.
[§] Ibid., vol. iii. p. 407.

on the introduction into the colony of every negro from abroad; and, although the alleged object of this statute was not the restriction of the slave-trade, but the payment of the colonial debt, yet so evidently would the former of these results follow, that the British crown, ever careful that nothing should impede this traffic, at once *vetoed the act.* *

The other attempt to restrict this trade was made in 1760. *"From prudential motives,"* the Assembly of South Carolina, at that time, passed an act forbidding the importation of any more slaves, into the colony. For once, at least, her eyes seem to have been opened to the greatness of this evil, and she was determined to rid herself of it. But this act, like every other one of a similar character through our entire colonial history, was immediately annulled by the royal veto, the governor reprimanded for having sanctioned such a bill, and the other colonies warned, by a circular letter, against similar offenses.†

With reference to the other colonies, it is hardly necessary that we should sketch, with any detail, their history. When Oglethorpe and his associates—seeking in this New World an asylum from the persecutions of the Old—settled Georgia, they determined forever to exclude slavery from that territory; and because of their obstinate adherence to this purpose, against the earnest remonstrance of the government at home, were deprived of their charter.‡ When Pennsylvania, in 1712, adopted "An Act to prevent the importation of negroes and Indians into her province," and, to make it effectual, imposed a heavy duty upon all such importations, the statute was immediately set aside by royal authority. When New Hampshire was separated from Massachusetts, and organized as a royal province, to prevent any imitation by her of that opposition to slavery that had from the very beginning distinguished the old Puritan colony, these instructions were given to her governor: " You are not to give your assent to, or pass any law imposing duties on negroes imported into New Hampshire."§ When Massachusetts, in 1774, brought a long series of legislative enactments against slavery to a close, by passing a bill, entitled "An Act to prevent the importations of negroes and others as slaves into this

---

* Bancroft, vol. iii. p. 329.

† Ibid., vol. iii. p. 416, and Princeton Repertory, July, 1862.

‡ Ibid., vol. iii. p. 416.

§ Gordon's American Revolution, vol. i. Letter 2.

province," Governor Hutchison not only vetoed the bill, but prorogued the Assembly;* and finally, in 1776, "amid all the agitations of the dawning revolution," the Earl of Dartmouth addressed to a colonial agent these memorable words, so truthfully expressive of what had been the whole policy of Great Britain to her American colonies : "*We cannot allow the colonies to check or discourage in any degree a traffic so beneficial to the nation.*"†

And here, with this history before us, it will be interesting, for one moment, to inquire into the cause of the pro-slavery policy of England, so persistently pursued toward her American colonies, for more than one hundred and fifty years ; for, if we mistake not, we shall discover in it, one great reason for her sympathy with those who are now seeking the dismemberment of our nation. England has, for several centuries, been a manufacturing nation, dependent to a great extent upon other countries, both for the supply of the raw material, and for a market for her finished wares. Whenever, then, her citizens emigrated to other lands, and English colonies were there formed, it was clearly for her interest that their inhabitants should be mainly engaged in agricultural pursuits. For should it be otherwise, should they become a manufacturing people, they would evidently be brought into competition with her. Planting colonies would minister to the wealth of England. They would, at the same time, be to her sources of supply, and channels for disbursement. Manufacturing colonies would tend to her poverty. They would lessen the demand for the products of her looms, by furnishing to the market their own goods.

But in no way could this end be better secured than by the establishment in her colonies of African slavery. Such an institution could hardly exist, save among an agricultural people. The intelligence and industry that successful manufacturing establishments require, are incompatible with labor that is constrained and uncompensated. A race scarcely half civilized, may, by the lash, be compelled to dig and to plow, but the task is not so easy when the labor is transferred from the field to the factory. Skillful artisans may, indeed, be occasionally found wearing the chains of slavery, but the instances are rare, and the experiment dangerous to a continued bondage. And, perhaps, we may here venture, without any fear of contradiction, to assert that a whole nation of artisans could not

---

* Princeton Repertory, July, 1862.
† Bancroft, vol. iii. p. 416.

be long retained in involuntary servitude. It was, therefore, to constrain the American colonies to become planting colonies, and thus guard her own manufactories from competition, that England sought so persistently to fill them with negroes.

And to the same cause, as we have already intimated, are we in a measure, to attribute England's sympathy in our day, with the great rebellion of the South. New England is a competitor of old England. By the cheapness, beauty, and durability of her manufactured fabrics, she has come to be a dangerous rival of the old country. Lowell and Lawrence, are beginning to stand by the side of Manchester and Stockport, and under the fostering care of a judicious protective tariff, may perhaps in the future race of trade even outrun them. Indeed, as an intelligent Englishman visits the eastern and northern sections of this country, he cannot, we think, fail to be deeply impressed with the, to him, *homelike* appearance of everything in the commercial life of this nation. In Pittsburg, begrimed with the dust and smoke of scores of furnaces, he sees his own Birmingham or Glasgow; Eastern Massachusetts, in whose villages and cities the hum of the spindle and the loom is almost unbroken, seems to him like a second Lancashire; and so vast a forest of masts as lie along, and stretch out from, the wharves of New York, he must remember scarce ever to have seen on the Thames, or the Mersey. But extending his journey to the cotton-growing States of the South, how different is the aspect of everything that he beholds! The picture is now one of contrast, not of resemblance. Nothing here in trade indicates any *competition* with his own country, but, on the contrary, everything denotes supply and demand. These States are, commercially, the correlative of England. They are *planting* States. They produce just what she needs to keep her factories in motion, and then aids in the consumption of her finished fabrics.

In her present sympathy, then, with the slaveholding interests of the South, England has only, we contend, been consistent with herself. It was to guard her own manufactories from competition, that she *forced the institution of slavery upon this land*. For this she planted this Upas in our country. And it is for this that she would protect and defend it, now that every fiber and leaf is quivering, under the vigorous blows of freedom.

And that the explanation just given of England's pro-slavery policy, toward her American colonies is the true one, the history of those times abundantly proves. A British merchant, in 1745, published a tract, entitled "The African Slave Trade the great Pillar and Support of the British Plantation Trade in America," from which Bancroft, in his History, makes the following quotation :—

"Were it possible for white men to answer the end of negroes in planting, the colonies would interfere with the manufactures of these kingdoms. In such case, indeed, we might have just reason to dread the prosperity of our colonies, but while we can supply them abundantly with negroes, we need be under no such apprehension. Negro labor will keep our British colonies in a due subserviency to the interest of their mother country; for while our plantations depend on planting by negroes, our colonies can never prove injurious to British manufactures, never become independent of these kingdoms."*

Nor is this the only evidence that we can adduce of the truthfulness of our position. One of the first articles that the colonists attempted to manufacture for themselves was iron. To this they were invited from their large necessities as a new people, and from the fact that the country especially abounded in this ore. And in time, they attained so much proficiency in this department of business, as not only to supply their own wants, but to export small quantities to England. But this fact at once excited alarm, and the subject proposed to the attention of the House of Commons, a committee was, in 1750, appointed *"To check the danger of American rivalry."* And the means, proposed by that committee, fell little short of positive prohibition. The bill introduced by them, and subsequently passed by the House, while it admitted American iron in its rudest form to be imported free of duty, "forbade the smiths of America to erect any mill for slitting or rolling iron, or any plating forge to work with a tilt-hammer, or any furnace for making steel." And at the very same time that these shackles for the labor of free men were forged, and England put her foot upon these nascent manufactories in her colonies, every restraint was taken away from the slave-trade, the whole coast of Africa, from Sallee to the Cape of Good Hope, was thrown open to all the subjects of the king, *"that the colonies might be filled with slaves, who would neither trouble Britain with fears of encouraging political independence, nor compete in their industry with British workshops."†*

---

* Bancroft, vol. iii. p. 416.
† Ibid., vol. iv. p. 62.

But we must hasten, to notice, another long series of facts, that are of the highest moment, to be known and remembered, by all who would fully understand the history of American slavery. *Closely connected in time with the purpose of our national independence, and its achievement, was the inauguration of an anti-slavery policy.*

This was just what might have been expected, upon the supposition, that we have truthfully portrayed the feelings that were generally prevalent on this subject, during our colonial history. The colonies opposed to the extension of slavery in their midst, and only prevented from successfully arresting its progress, by the interposition of royal authority; the conclusion is irresistible that with that authority denied, and successfully resisted, the inception of emancipation would immediately follow. And so it was. Between the years 1777 and 1804, eight out of the thirteen colonies provided, by special legislative enactments, for the entire extinction, throughout their whole territory, of slavery. And that the remainder did not follow so goodly an example, is to be explained by the fact, that the slave-trade had been in them so effectually plied as, in a measure, to subdue that opposition to slavery which had once been so general. We say "in a measure" subdued it, for even in some of these colonies, we find legislative acts proposed or adopted, that were directly intended to arrest the progress of slavery, and thus prepare the way for its final abolition. Especially was this true of the Virginia colony, in whose soil this institution was, as we have seen, first planted. In October, 1778, the General Assembly of Virginia passed an act, declaring that "*no slave should thereafter be brought into this commonwealth* by land or by water, and that every slave imported contrary thereto, should upon such importation be free."* Here both the domestic, and foreign slave-trade were, by statute, positively prohibited. Every channel of supply was cut off. The new Constitution, also, for Virginia, prepared and proposed by Jefferson a few years subsequent to this, contained a provision, by which all born after the year 1800 should be free.† And it was with reference to this proposition that Washington, in writing to his nephew, Lawrence Lewis, in August, 1797, says: "I wish from my soul that the legislature of this State could see the policy of a gradual abolition of

---

* Tucker's Blackstone, vol. ii. p. 47, Appendix.
† Stroud's Laws of Slavery, p. 6.

slavery.   It might prevent much future mischief."* And, though
this clause of the constitution was finally rejected, yet how expressive of the true anti-slavery feeling that then pervaded Virginia is
the fact, asserted by Jefferson, that 10,000 slaves were voluntarily
emancipated in that State during the first ten years of our existence as an independent people !†

Maryland, also, in 1783 prohibited the further importation of
slaves into her territory, and removed all legal restrictions on
emancipation ; and three years later, in 1786, North Carolina declared the introduction of slaves into that State "of evil consequence and highly impolitic," and imposed a duty of five pounds
on each slave thus imported.‡

But it is not in the acts of the separate States, or colonies *only*,
that, coeval with the purpose and achievement of our independence, we can see the inception of an anti-slavery policy.   It is
readily discovered in the first Congress of Delegates, in the Convention that framed our Constitution, and in the early sessions of
our Federal Congress.   Among the first measures adopted by the
Congress of Delegates, which commenced its sessions in Philadelphia on the 5th of September, 1774, and which was, let it be
remembered, the first representative body of the colonies, was—as
one of the articles of the non-importation agreement—a solemn
pledge to abstain from, and discountenance the slave-trade.§   And,
as if this single act was insufficient, or might be overlooked in the
details with which it was there connected, the pledge was afterward changed into a positive prohibition.   On the 6th of April,
1776, it was resolved that no slaves be imported into any of the
thirteen colonies.‖   And so, again, when in 1787—the same year
in which the Federal Constitution was framed—Virginia ceded the
territory northwest of the Ohio River to the "Confederation,"the
condition of its acceptance by the Continental Congress was, that
slavery should never be permitted there.   And the insertion of this
condition in the ordinance, not only secured the vote of all the Southern States then represented in Congress, but, according to Mr.
Benton, it was "*pre-eminently the work of the South.*"   "The

---

* Irving's Washington, vol. v. p. 299.
† Twenty-First Report of Pennsylvania Anti-Slavery Society, p. 7.
‡ Political Text Book, p. 50.
§ Elliot's Debates on the Federal Constitution, vol. i. p. 44.
‖ Ibid., p. 54.

ordinance for the government of the territory was reported by a committee of five members, of whom three were from slaveholding States, and two—and one of them the chairman—were from Virginia alone."* Indeed, that the great *conception* of prohibiting slavery in that territory belongs to Jefferson, there can be no doubt.†

And that a similar policy, was *designed* to be pursued, by the framers of our Federal Constitution, we are constrained to believe. The idea, that that instrument should ever become the great bulwark of slavery in this land, perpetuating its existence where already established, and promoting its extension into new territories, would have been most abhorrent, to a large majority of those who assisted in its construction. In their earnest desire, to compact into one united and harmonious government, States so widely separated from each other in social institutions, and geographical boundaries; they did indeed give, in the formation of the Constitution, certain advantages to slavery, which we now cannot but deeply regret; but it was all with the conviction, that the system would certainly pass away, before the advancing power of civilization and freedom. Moreover, it is to be remembered that when the Constitution of the United States was formed, slavery had been abolished in but *four*, of the thirteen States, that were then confederated.

In judging of the true spirit of any assembly of men, it is likewise obvious, that we must look not simply at the conclusions to which the majority reached, but also at the whole history of the discussions which may have preceded these conclusions, and at the peculiar circumstances which may have favored them. A judgment formed, entirely apart from such considerations, may clearly be entirely erroneous. Let us apply this principle to the case before us.

It is well known that our Constitution contains three provisions with reference to slavery, though the word itself never occurs in the whole instrument. It provides, that three-fifths of those who are held in slavery, shall be included within the enumeration of inhabitants, by which the ratio of representation is determined; (Article I. Section 2;) it forbade the prohibiting by Congress of the slave-trade prior to the year 1808, (Article I. Section 9;) and

---

* Thirty Years in the United States Senate, vol. i. pp. 133, 134.
† Stroud's Laws of Slavery, p. 118.

it provides for the rendition of persons "held to service or labor
in one State, under the laws thereof," who have escaped "into
another," (Article IV. Section 2.)

I. With regard to the first of these provisions, we concede that
it was a lamentable concession to slavery, and likewise that it has
been the cause of incalculable injury to this nation. No argument
can defend it. The legislative representation of slaves, by their
masters, is a monstrous anomaly in a republican government.
But, conceding all this, does it follow that, in the introduction of
this provision into the Constitution, its framers designed to make
that instrument pro-slavery, either in its spirit or influence? It
is to be remembered, that the question which most profoundly agitated that Convention, was the apportionment of the congressional
representatives among the several States. Some contended for an
equality of representation, such as was secured to them by the
old "Articles of Confederation;" others demanded that the representation should be in proportion either to wealth or population.
The discussion was long and violent. Threats were added to
arguments. Some of the smaller States talked of "foreign powers
who would take them by the hand,"* should the Convention de-
termine upon an inequality of suffrage. Franklin, almost in despair
of human help, moved that hereafter the Convention, every morning, implore the Divine blessing upon its deliberations, and enforced his motion by this weighty inquiry: "As a sparrow does
not fall without Divine permission, can we suppose that govern-
ments are ever erected without His will?"† Indeed, during the
fortnight that was spent in the discussion of this subject, the
Convention was, in the language of one of its own members, "on
the *very verge of dissolution.*" It was "*scarce held together by
the strength of a hair.*"‡ And finally a harmonious conclusion
was reached *only* by mutual concessions. The larger States consented to an *equal* representation in the Senate; the smaller
States to an *unequal* representation in the House of Representatives. And, as in the case of the large slaveholding States, the
white population was small in comparison with that which the
large free States contained, the equality of representation between
the two, was sought to be promoted by adding, in the former instances, to the enumeration of the free inhabitants, three-fifths of

---

* Elliot's Debates on the Federal Constitution, vol. i. p. 473.
† Ibid., p. 460.   ‡ Ibid., p. 358.

all other persons. Thus, it was entirely as a *compromise*, and one, too, deemed at the time essential to the formation of any federative system, that this provision was introduced into our Constitution.

But though such was its character, let no one imagine that it was permitted to pass, in silence, that body. The very men who finally voted for it, as a concession necessary or expedient to be made, still declared, in the most stirring words, their faith in its unrighteousness. An address delivered before the legislature of Maryland, by Luther Martin, Esq., Attorney-General of the State, and one of its delegates to the Convention that framed the Federal Constitution, contains this remarkable paragraph :—

" With respect to that part of the second section of the first article, which relates to the apportionment of representation and direct taxation, there were considerable objections made to it, besides the great objection of inequality. It was urged, that no principle could justify taking slaves into computation in apportioning the number of representatives a State should have in the Government ; that it involved the absurdity of increasing the power of a State in making laws for *free men* in proportion as that State violated the rights of freedom ; that it might be proper to take slaves into consideration when taxes were to be apportioned, because it had a tendency to discourage slavery ; but to take them into account in giving representation, tended to *continue* that infamous traffic ; that slaves could not be taken into account as men, or citizens, because they were not admitted to the rights of citizens in the States which adopted or continued slavery. If they were to be taken into account as property, it was asked what peculiar circumstance should render this property (of all others the most odious in its nature) entitled to the high privilege of conferring consequence and power in the Government to its possessors, rather than any other property ? and why slaves should, as property, be taken into account rather than horses, cattle, mules, or any other species ? And it was observed, by an honorable member from Massachusetts, that he considered it as dishonorable and humiliating to enter into compact with the slaves of the Southern States, as it would with the *horses* and *mules* of the Eastern."*

---

* Elliot's Debates on the Federal Constitution, vol. i. p. 363.

It may be worthy of remark, in this connection, as illustrating the general truth of our position, that, although the " member from Massachusetts" opposed so strenuously by his speech this provision of the Constitution, yet by his vote he supported it. The principle was first introduced by a resolution moved by James Wilson, of Pennsylvania, June 11, 1787. Massachusetts voted in the affirmative. (*Ibid.*, vol. i. 169.)

II. With regard to the constitutional provision that "the migration or importation of such persons as any of the States now existing shall think proper to admit, shall not be prohibited by Congress prior to 1808"—the second reference, as we have seen, that that instrument makes to slavery—there are several things that should be said. (*a*) It did not preclude, but implied, the right of the States severally to prohibit the importation of slaves in their own domain. (*b*) It did not prevent Congress at any time from excluding the traffic from the territories. (*c*) It was a virtual concession of the iniquity of the trade; it set the seal of the country's reprobation upon it. (*d*) In a measure it foreshadowed its coming end. To say that prior to 1808 Congress shall not prohibit in any State the slave-trade, is almost tantamount to saying that after that it may, and, in all probability, will. It was a sure prophecy of its destruction.

Moreover, from the history of the Convention we learn that the introduction of this provision into the Constitution, was the result of a compromise between the clashing interests of commerce and slavery. When the first draft of the Constitution was reported, (August 6, 1787,) it contained one section, (Article VII. Section 4,) which entirely forbade Congress at any time from prohibiting the slave-trade, and another, which provided (Article VII. Section 6) that "No navigation act should be passed without the assent of two-thirds of the members present in each house."* The former of these sections the South were solicitous to retain; the latter the North were as anxious to reject. The one fostered slavery, the other would cripple commerce. The result that was finally reached through a committee appointed "to reconcile these conflicting interests," was the entire omission of the section restricting navigation acts, and the amendment of that which related to the importation of slaves, so as to limit, to a certain specified time, its prohibition by Congress.† A member of that committee thus speaks of its deliberations: "I found the *Eastern States*, notwithstanding their *aversion to slaves*, very willing to indulge the Southern States, at least with a temporary liberty to prosecute the slave-trade; provided the Southern States would, in their turn, gratify *them* by laying no restriction on navigation acts; and after a very little while the committee, by a great majority, agreed to such a report."‡

---

* Elliot's Debates on the Federal Constitution, vol. i. p. 227.
† Ibid., p. 261.   ‡ Ibid., p. 373.

But it was not without considerable opposition that this report received the sanction of the Convention. Indeed, there is hardly anything in the whole history of that body more worthy of remark than the bold attacks upon slavery which were made in connection with that discussion. "In a government formed *pretendedly* on the principles of liberty, and for its preservation, to have a provision, not only putting it out of its power at once to restrain and prevent the slave trade, but even encouraging that infamous traffic, ought," it was contended, "to be considered as a solemn mockery of, and insult to that God whose protection we had implored; and could not fail to hold us up in detestation, and render us contemptible to every true friend of liberty in the world." * * "Slavery" was alleged to be "inconsistent with the genius of republicanism, and has a tendency to destroy those principles on which it is supported." * * It was likewise urged that "national crimes can only be, and frequently are, punished in this world by national judgments, and that the continuance of the slave-trade, and thus giving it a national *sanction* and encouragement, ought to be considered as justly exposing us to the displeasure and vengeance of Him who is equally Lord of all, and who views with equal eye the poor African slave and his American master."* Nor was this opposition confined to the non-slaveholding States. The vote of Virginia was uniformly against this provision of the Constitution;† and the fact of its existence in that instrument was employed as an argument for its rejection before the Legislature of Maryland. "You will perceive, Sir," said Luther Martin, in the address already referred to, "not only that the general government is prohibited from interfering in the slave-trade before the year 1808, but that there is no provision in the Constitution that it shall afterwards be prohibited, nor any security that such prohibition will ever take place! and I think there is great reason to believe that, if the importation of slaves is permitted until the year 1808, it will not be prohibited afterwards. *At this time we do not generally hold this commerce in so great abhorrence* as we have done. When our liberties were at stake, we warmly felt for the common rights of men. The danger being thought to be past which threatened ourselves, we are daily growing more insensible to those rights."‡

---

* Elliot's Debates on the Federal Constitution, vol. i. pp. 373, 374.
† Ibid., vol. i. p. 265.
‡ Ibid., vol. i. pp. 374, 375.

III. Of that provision of the Constitution which relates to the rendition of fugitive slaves, the question has been much agitated, whether its intent was to clothe Congress with the power of legislating in respect to the surrender of such persons, or whether it was intended to leave it to the several States to provide a mode for the investigation of such claims, and, if found for the claimants, to deliver up to them the fugitives. That regarding alone the letter of the provision, it is, at least, susceptible of this latter interpretation, few, we suppose, would deny. It was thus that Daniel Webster, the greatest Constitutional lawyer of his age, if not of our country, understood it, and the fact that it was adopted by the unanimous vote of the Convention certainly favors such interpretation. Although, then, the Supreme Court of the United States has set this question, *legally*, at rest, by deciding that the *power* of legislating with respect to fugitive slaves belongs *exclusively* to the Federal government;* and though that government has, in accordance with this decision, frequently legislated upon the subject, yet for no one of these acts, whatever may be their character, can the Constitution be *certainly* held responsible. No one can positively affirm that the framers of that instrument ever designed to confer such authority. All for which it can *properly* be held responsible is the simple fact of the return to bondage of those who may have escaped from it. And if free and slave States are in any way to confederate, is not such a provision essential? Where the territory of freedom is continuous to that of slavery, can the line of demarkation be preserved distinct, save by some arrangement that will prevent liberty from being secured by its simple passage? The injustice of the rendition of fugitive slaves in States confederated under one government, lies not in the *fact* of the rendition, for which the Constitution alone provides, but in the *mode* by which that end is secured, by special legislative enactments.

And a similar anti-slavery policy can easily be traced through the first sessions of our Federal Congress. Men utterly ignore the *early* history of our national government, who suppose that its power was employed in conserving, and upholding slavery. The very reverse was true. Many solemn acts of legislation, sanctioned by every branch of our national administration, were passed, with the avowed purpose of restricting, limiting, and ultimately destroying this institution. The fathers of our republic were per-

---

* 16 Peters, pp. 539, 622.

sistent in their efforts to curtail, and finally to destroy the *slave-trade*. They sought entirely to dry up the fountain of this evil, to cut off the source of its supply, and thus, in time, to secure liberty to the whole land. Let us verify this assertion by a brief record of facts.

Two years after the adoption of our Federal Constitution by Conventions of the several States, Congress *prohibited the foreign slave-trade*. On the 22d of March, 1794, an act was passed, declaring that "no citizen or resident of the country should build, equip, or send out any ship or vessel to any foreign country to procure the inhabitants thereof, or to transport them to any *foreign place* or *port* to be sold or disposed of as slaves." And the penalty annexed to this statute was the confiscation of the vessel, and a fine of $200 for each person so taken or sold. And here, it is well to remark, that this act was passed *thirteen years* before a similar policy was established by the English government. Instead, therefore, of being constrained by the sentiment of other nations to assume this position, it was in advance of that sentiment, and tended to create it. We were not here the slow imitators of others, but rather the noble exemplar, that they have tardily followed.

And, that this act might be still more effectual in the destruction of the foreign slave-trade, it was, on the 10th of May, 1800, supplemented by another, which declared " that no citizen or resident of the United States should own, or have any right of property in any ship or vessel engaged in the slave-trade anywhere upon the sea, no matter from what place or port it might sail." This act was also enforced by new and more severe penalties. "It prohibited any sailor from serving on board of a slaver, and authorized our commissioned vessels to seize any ship engaged in this trade, and bring her into port for condemnation."

Nor was it the *foreign slave-trade alone* that our national Congress in its earlier sessions sought to destroy. Unable, as we have seen, prior to 1808, by a special provision of the Constitution, to prohibit "the migration or importation of such persons as any of the *States* now existing shall think proper to admit," it yet had the right of such a prohibition with reference to the *Territories*, and did not scruple, in some instances, to exercise it. On the 7th of April, 1798, an act was passed by Congress, authorizing the establishment of a government in the Mississippi Territory, the 7th section of which provides "That after the establishment of the aforesaid government it shall not be lawful for any person or persons to import or bring into the said Mississippi Territory, from any port or place *without* the limits of the United States, or to cause to be imported * * any slave or slaves, and that every person so offending * * shall forfeit * * for each slave so imported * * the sum of $300 * * and that every slave so imported shall thereupon become entitled to, and receive his or her freedom."* And the provision of a similar nature, incorporated into the Act of Congress, passed March 26th, 1804, entitled "An Act erecting Louisiana into two territories, and providing for the temporary government thereof," is still more hostile to slavery. It prohibits the introduction into Louisiana Territory "from any port or place *within*," as well as without "the limits of the United States * * *any slave or slaves* which had been imported since the first of May, 1798, into any port or place within the limits of the United States, or which should be imported thereafter." And contains, in addition, this provision, "And no slave or slaves shall directly or indirectly be introduced into said territory, except by a citizen of the United States removing into said territory *for actual settlement*, and being at the time of such removal *bona fide owner* of such slave or slaves; and every slave imported or brought into the said territory, contrary to the provisions of this act, shall thereupon be entitled to and receive his freedom."†

But these attempts to destroy the slave trade abroad, and to curtail it at home, were only preliminary to its entire prohibition ; and it is an interesting fact that that was decreed at the very earliest day on which Congress had the power. On the second of March, 1807, it was enacted "that from and after January 1, 1808, it shall not be lawful to import or bring into the United States, or the territories thereof, from any foreign kingdom, place, or country, any negro, mulatto, or person of color as a slave, or to be held to service and labor." The penalty incurred for a violation of this statute was the confiscation of the vessel, and a fine of $20,000 each against the parties engaged, their aiders and abettors. To enforce it, the President was also empowered to employ the naval forces of the nation.

By a subsequent act this penalty was increased. Imprisonment was added to fines, and the forfeiture of property. On the 20th of

---

* Acts of the 2d Session of the Fifth Congress, ch. 45.
† 2 Story's Laws, p. 937.

April, 1818, Congress passed a statute providing that all persons convicted of being in any way engaged in the slave-trade should "be imprisoned for a term not exceeding seven years, nor less than three years." And finally, as a fitting conclusion to this policy, so persistently pursued through a long course of years, Congress, on the 15th of May, 1820, declared the slave-trade, and the act of detaining negroes or mulattoes, with intent to make them slaves, to be *piracy*, and provided that any person whatever who should engage in the trade, or assist in detaining such persons, with the intent to make them slaves, should be adjudged a *pirate, and as such shall suffer death.*

But this brings us to the last point in the history of American Slavery that we propose in this article to notice. *Its defenders are entirely of modern times.* The idea that the involuntary servitude of reasonable beings, except as a punishment for crime, was indefensibly wrong, was, until a little more than a quarter of a century ago, almost universal; and in respect to the existence of such a servitude *here*, it was, until the time just mentioned, everywhere spoken of as a great moral and political evil.

In confirmation of this position, it is pertinent to refer to the whole series of facts just detailed; for surely men who, by legislative enactments continued for a long course of years, sought to limit, curtail, and ultimately destroy the institution of slavery, could not have regarded it, as either morally right or politically expedient. We are not wont to dry up a fountain, when we believe that the streams which issue from it, flow out in blessings to the world; nor do we lay the axe at the root of a tree whose fruit we know to be pleasant and healthful. If men believed that the introduction of a single slave into this land was a crime against humanity, worthy of death, and if they were ready to embody that faith in a positive statute, how could they regard as innocent his continuance in bondage, and the entail of servitude upon his latest posterity? The importation into this country of Africans, as slaves, a wrong, so deep that *blood* alone could atone for it, the wrong of holding them hopelessly and forever in that relation is, from the premise, we contend, a logical conclusion. True, a wise expediency and a due regard to Christ's great law of love, may not demand their *immediate enfranchisement.* Strangers in a strange land, and savages in the midst of civilization, such a course *might* only deepen the wrong that they have already suf-

fered. With the intent of preparing them for freedom, its enjoy-
ment might *rightfully be temporarily denied them.*

Precisely this was the view of American slavery that, until quite
recently, was universally cherished in this land. Those honored men
of our nation who stood up, as we have seen, so boldly in their opposition to the slave-trade, who branded it as inhuman and infamous,
who first fined, and then imprisoned, and then pronounced as worthy
of death, all who were in any way engaged in it, were not so illog-
ical as to fail to see the true scope and bearing of their acts. No!
They saw it, and meant that the world should see it. Their severe
condemnation of the slave-trade, and their persistent efforts to destroy it, was the purposed avowal of their faith, that every system
of involuntary servitude that was not designed to ultimate in universal freedom, and that was not conducted so as certainly to secure
this end, was indefensibly wrong.

But it is not upon any inference alone, however logical, that we
rest our position. The frequent introduction of slavery, as a topic
of earnest discussion, in our National Congress, was one of the
unavoidable results of its existence. The feature of society that
distinguished one portion of our Union from the other, and that
caused the interests of one section to conflict with those of the
other, there was in fact scarcely a single question of national policy,
that was not in some measure complicated with it, and that conse-
quently did not involve its consideration. And surely if, in any
place, and under any circumstances, slavery would find valiant
defenders, here is the place and the occasion. Men, we know, in
the heat of debate and under the irritation of opposing sentiments,
often go much further in the statement of their own, than their
cooler judgment would allow. In reading, then, the discussions
of slavery that were had in the early sessions of our National Congress, how natural the expectation that we would find *there*, if
anywhere, this institution, in its righteousness and humanity,
stoutly defended. *But it is not so.* Southern statesmen, in those
days, were indeed often earnest in the maintenance of those rights
which they supposed the Constitution secured to their peculiar
institution, but *seldom if ever*, did they boldly avow it to be in
itself just and humane. Their more general policy was frankly to
acknowledge slavery as an evil, for the present to be borne pa-
tiently and kindly, but in the future *to be, in some way unseen by
them, forever abolished.*

From the many illustrations of this truth which might be given we will select two, not because they are any more striking than many others, but because they are in time the nearest that we can discover to that most lamentable change of sentiment which on this subject has recently taken place.

One of the most earnest, protracted, and exciting debates that ever took place in our National Congress, was in connection with the admission of Missouri as a State into the Federal Union. Commencing as early as April, 1818, it was continued until the commencement of 1821, and was oftentimes conducted with so much acrimony and sectional jealousy, as to threaten the very stability of the government. Jefferson, the sun of whose life was then near its setting, was greatly alarmed, and frequently expressed his fear that that union of States, which he had done so much to form, was on the eve of dissolution. And, indeed, had it not been for what is usually called the "Missouri Compromise," we can hardly see how such a catastrophe could have been avoided. By that act mutual concessions were made; nor is it easy to see which party was really the gainer. Missouri, admitted as a slaveholding State into the Union, slavery was, on the other hand, forever prohibited from an extent of territory larger than the area of all the Atlantic Slave States put together. Moreover, it is to be remembered that, contemporaneous with this act, was the admission of Maine as a free State, and also that treaty which, in acquiring Florida, ceded Texas, the largest possession of the United States south of the proposed line, to Spain. Mr. Benton is doubtless mistaken in asserting that this "compromise" was "all clear gain to the anti-slavery side of the question;"* or, again, that "it yielded forever to the free States the absolute predominance in the Union."† But no less in error we think, are those who, on the other side, regard it as a signal triumph of slavery over freedom. It was emphatically a "compromise."

But what in this protracted and earnest discussion most concerns us here to notice, is the almost entire absence of any defense of slavery, either upon moral or political grounds. The men who so persistently demanded that no restrictions should be put upon slavery in Missouri, founded their argument almost entirely upon those rights which the Constitution secured to the separate States.

---

* Benton's Thirty Years in the U. S. Senate, vol. i. p. 5.
† Ibid., vol. ii. p. 140.

They did not contend that slavery should be extended because it was a good institution, approved of God, and fraught with blessings to society. The very reverse was true. They acknowledged it as an evil, apologized for its existence in their midst, condemned the whole system as essentially unrighteous, and expressed their confident hope that the institution would in time be entirely removed from our land. How remarkable this fact! That no one may be skeptical as to its truthfulness, let us quote a few sentences from several of the memorable speeches that were then made. "Sir! I envy," said John Randolph, "neither the head nor the heart of any man from the North who rises here to defend slavery." "Slavery was *an evil*," said Senator Elliott, of Georgia, found in this country at the formation of the present government, and it was *tolerated*, only because it could not be remedied."* "Gentlemen tell us," said Mr. Lowrie, of Pennsylvania, "that slavery is *an evil, and that they lament its existence*, and yet, strange as it may seem, they contend for the extension of this evil to the peaceful regions west of the Mississippi."† "Many of those who have opposed this amendment," said John Sergeant, of Pennsylvania— that is, the amendment prohibiting slavery from Missouri—"have agreed with us in characterizing slavery *as an evil and a curse*, in language stronger than we should perhaps be at liberty to use."‡

A writer in Niles' Register for March 11, 1820, reviewing the whole debate on this subject, says: "Few, if any, are bold enough to advocate the practice of slavery as being right in itself, or dare to justify it, except on the plea of necessity." Indeed, Mr. Clay, in his celebrated speech near the close of this discussion, ventured to rebuke his Southern brethren for conceding so frankly the unrighteousness of slavery, characterizing it as an "unnecessary concession." Nor should we here fail to mention, as illustrating still further how almost universally prevalent anti-slavery sentiments then were, the fact, that in connection with this great debate, the legislatures of New York, Pennsylvania, and New Jersey, all *unanimously* passed resolutions, not only objecting to the admission of Missouri as a slaveholding State into the Union, but objecting hereafter to the admission of any territory as a State, without making the prohibition of slavery an indispensable condition of its admission.§

---

* Niles' Register, vol. xvii. p. 408.   † Ibid., vol. xvii. p. 415.
‡ Ibid., vol. xviii. p. 382.   § Political Text-Book, p. 60.

The other Congressional debate that I have selected as illustrating this truth, occurred in the Senate about nine years after the one we have just noticed, and has been made especially memorable by the well-known reply of Webster to Hayne. The discussion did not in itself involve the subject of slavery. It arose upon a motion to limit the sales of the public lands; but as this naturally led to some comparison between the growth of free and slave territory, a debate upon the whole subject soon followed; and, for many reasons, the discussion was one peculiarly irritating to the South. It came upon them unexpectedly; was not really germain to the subject; seemed to be introduced for the very purpose of provoking reply and stirring up anger; and contained many incontrovertible facts, that were most damaging to slavery. Thus,.comparing Kentucky and Ohio, Mr. Webster attributed the superior improvement and population of the latter, to its exemption from the evils of slavery, and with this as an example, generalized, to what must always be the effect in any State, of its permission or prohibition. In reply, the principal speakers were Mr. Hayne, of South Carolina, and Mr. Benton, of Missouri, and though they both resented, with warmth, as a reflection upon the Slave States, this disadvantageous comparison, they still essayed no defense of slavery, but, on the contrary, fully and freely admitted it to be a great evil. The spirit of their speeches was, in this regard, precisely like that which characterized—as we have already seen—the debate on the Missouri controversy. We extract a few sentences from one of the speeches of Mr. Benton, which will not only confirm our present position, but throw light upon others that we have previously in this article considered. Addressing himself to the North, and declaring his purpose "to disabuse them of some erroneous impressions," Mr. Benton remarks:—

"To them I can truly say that slavery, *in the abstract*, has but few advocates or defenders in the slaveholding States, and that slavery *as it is*, an hereditary institution descended upon us from our ancestors, would have fewer advocates among us than it has, if those who have nothing to do with the subject would only let us alone. * * The views of *leading men in the North and the South were indisputably the same in the earlier periods of our government.* Of this our legislative history contains the highest proof. The foreign slave-trade was prohibited in Virginia as soon as the Revolution began. It was one of her first acts of sovereignty. In the convention of that State which adopted the Federal Constitution, it was an objection to that instrument that it tolerated the African slave-trade for twenty years. Nothing that has appeared since has surpassed the indignant denunciations of this traffic by Patrick Henry, George Mason, and others in that convention."*

But from this view of what, until quite recently, was the anti-slavery sentiment of this country, as evinced by the spirit of our Congressional debates, let us now for one moment turn to observe the same fact as illustrated by the deliverances of different religious bodies.

Slavery, a moral question, and having so many points of practical contact with the Church, nothing is more natural than the supposition that it would oftentimes find its way into the Church's highest convocations, and constrain from them some expression of opinion as to its true character. And though these deliverances do not certainly indicate the general sentiment that might at the time prevail, yet are they the true exponents of the Church's feeling, and with this it is reasonable to infer that most good men agreed. What, then, has the Church of Christ in former times said of this institution? What opinion of its moral character has she solemnly promulgated? We well know that *now*, and for some years past, large bodies of professed Christians in this land, have given to slavery their unqualified approval. They have pronounced their solemn benediction upon it. They have dared to speak of it as a divine institution, fraught with blessings to both of the parties between whom it subsists, and destined to continue until the latest generation. How startling the contrast between these deliverances of the modern Church, and those in which our fathers and *theirs* once all together united! The following minute was adopted by the Conference of the Methodist Episcopal Church in 1784:—

"Every member in our Society who has slaves in those States where the law will admit of freeing them, shall, after notice given him by the preacher, set them free within twelve months, (except in Virginia, and there within two years,) at specified periods, according to age. Every person concerned who will not comply with these rules, shall have liberty to withdraw within twelve months after the notice is given, otherwise to be excluded. No person holding slaves shall in future be admitted into the Society until he previously comply with these rules respecting slavery."†

And though at a subsequent Conference these regulations were

---

* Benton's Thirty Years in the U. S. Senate, vol. i. p. 136.
† Lee's History of the Methodists.

suspended, yet in 1797 this paragraph was added to the Discipline of that denomination:—

"The preachers and other members of our Society are requested to consider the subject of negro slavery with deep attention, and that they impart to the General Conference, through the medium of the Yearly Conference, or otherwise, any important thoughts on the subject, that the Conference may have full light, in order to take further steps toward eradicating this enormous evil from that part of the Church of Christ and God with which they are connected."*

At a meeting of the General Committee of the *Baptists* of Virginia, in 1789, the following resolution was adopted:—

"Resolved, That slavery is a violent deprivation of the rights of nature, and inconsistent with republican government, and therefore we recommend it to our brethren to make use of every measure to extirpate this horrid evil from the land, and pray Almighty God that our honorable legislature may have it in their power to proclaim this great jubilee, consistent with the principles of good policy."†

The General Synod of the Presbyterian Church, as early as 1787, recommended "in the warmest terms to every member of that body, and to all the churches and families under their care, to do everything in their power, consistent with the rights of civil society, to promote the *abolition of slavery*, and the instruction of negroes, whether bond or free;" and four years after the organization of the first General Assembly, (1793,) that body expressed their approbation of this action, by ordering that it be published in their minutes.‡ Two years later than this (1795) the General Assembly assured "all the churches under their care that they viewed with the deepest concern any vestiges of slavery which may exist in this country;"§ and subsequently (1815) "expressed their regret that the slavery of Africans and their descendants still continues in so many places, and even among those within the bounds of the church."‖ In 1818, the same body "having taken into consideration the subject of slavery," thus "make known their" UNANIMOUS "sentiments upon it to the churches and people under their care."

" We consider the voluntary enslaving of one part of the human race by another as a gross violation of the most precious and sacred rights of

---

* Benezet, Views of Slavery, p. 102.   † Ibid., p. 103.
‡ Assembly's Digest, p. 268.   § Ibid., p. 269.
‖ Ibid., p. 271.

human nature, as utterly inconsistent with the law of God, which requires
us to love our neighbor as ourselves, and as totally unreconcilable with
the spirit and principles of the Gospel of Christ, which enjoin that 'All
things whatsoever ye would that men should do to you, do ye even so to
them.'   *   *   *   We rejoice that the Church to which we belong commenced as early as any other in this country the good work of endeavor-
ing to put an end to slavery, and that in the same work many of its members have ever since been, and now are among the most active, vigorous,
and efficient laborers.   *   *   *   We earnestly exhort them to continue,
and, if possible, to increase their exertion, to effect the total abolition of
slavery."*

Nor were these solemn denunciations of the sin of slavery confined to the highest judicatory of the church, where, it might be
said, that Northern influence prevailed.   The Synod of Kentucky,
in 1835, appointed a committee " to digest and prepare a plan for
the moral and religious instruction of our slaves, and for their
future emancipation," and in their report, adopted the year following, such declarations as these occur:—

" We *all* admit that the system of slavery, which exists among us, is
not right.†   *   *   Without any crime on the part of its unfortunate
subjects, they are deprived for life, and their posterity after them, of the
right to property, of the right to liberty, of the right to personal security.
These odious features are not the excrescences upon the system, they are
the system itself; they are its essential constituent parts.   And can any
man believe that any such a thing as this is not sinful, that it is not hated
by God, and ought not to be abhorred and abolished by man ?‡   *   *   *
This work must be done, or wrath will come upon us.   The groans of
millions do not rise forever unheeded before the throne of the Almighty.
The hour of doom must soon arrive, the storm must soon gather, the bolt
of destruction must soon be hurled, and the guilty must soon be dashed
in pieces.   The voice of history and the voice of inspiration both warn us
that the catastrophe must come, unless averted by repentance."§

Such, then, *until quite recently*, was public opinion in this
country upon the subject of slavery, as manifested, in the spirit of
our Congressional debates, and in the deliverances of the Christian
Church.   Indeed, a distinguished jurist, whose researches upon this
subject entitle his opinion to peculiar weight, says, "About the year

---

* Assembly's Digest, pp. 272, 273.
† Enormity of the Slave-trade, p. 76.
‡ Ibid., p. 81.
§ Ibid., p. 108.

1830, for the first time, so far as my information extends, among men of the least political repute, it was announced by a Governor of South Carolina that the institution of slavery was eminently useful and beneficent."*

Should there be any exception to this remark, many things, which we need not here stop particularly to mention, would point to Mr. Calhoun, the distinguished senator of the same State. The "Magnus Apollo" of slavery in these later days, it is difficult to think of him as anything else than its stout defender. And yet so it was. Mr. Calhoun did not always think that American slavery was a benign institution, and that it should be perpetuated in this land. He was a convert, like all his other brethren at the South, to a new doctrine on this subject. Of this fact, one of his speeches in the Senate, in 1838, contains almost a confession: "Many," he says, "in the South once believed that slavery was a moral and political evil, but that folly and delusion are gone. We now see it in its true light, and regard it as the most safe and stable basis for free institutions." A member of President Monroe's cabinet, when the Missouri Compromise was proposed, Mr. Calhoun also gave to that measure his cordial approbation;† and as late as 1837 declared in the Senate "that it was due to candor to say that his impressions were in its favor."‡

A recent writer thus reports a conversation that this distinguished Southerner had, "more than twenty years ago," with "a philosophic observer, never absorbed in politics, and who visited Washington as a young man with good introductions, after his return from a long tour of observation in Europe."

"Sir, people believe that I am an unqualified advocate of slavery—that I hold the institution to be permanent and just. This, sir, is an error. I have no faith in slavery as a *permanent* institution, nor as a *true one*. I believe it to be but temporary, it serves a present purpose; it is very important to maintain it while it serves this purpose, and for this reason I defend and uphold it; but I am no believer in, no *advocate of slavery* in itself; it is an institution which is destined to come to an end and disappear, like so many others, after having fulfilled its mission."§

* Stroud's Laws of Slavery, Preface to Second Edition, p. 6.
† Benton's Thirty Years in U S. Senate, vol. i. p. 744.
‡ Ibid., vol. ii. p. 136.
§ Independent, December 25th, 1862.

But this is not all.   There is a fact in the life of Mr. Calhoun, remarkable in itself, and in the highest degree pertinent to the point we are now illustrating, that recently came to the knowledge of the writer of this article, and though no public announcement of it may have ever, before this, been made, yet of its truthfulness there can be no doubt. While on a visit to the North, in the summer of 1821 or 1822, Mr. Calhoun was frequently in the society of an eminent Presbyterian divine.   The acquaintance that had for many years existed between the two men, invited in their interviews the fullest and frankest expressions of opinion, and this was doubtless still further promoted by their entire diversity of pursuits. The theme that engrossed a large part of their conversation was naturally the institution of American slavery, for in the admission of Missouri as a slaveholding State into the Union, we had just as a nation came through our first great struggle on that subject. In everything, however, that was said upon this theme, Mr. Calhoun attempted no defense of the system, but, on the contrary, unhesitatingly pronounced it to be a great evil, both morally and politically.   At these declarations the divine expressed surprise, and urged that the distinguished Southerner, as he was certainly greatly misunderstood on this subject, should give to them some public expression. And as a definite mode, he suggested the preparation by him of a bill for the abolition of slavery, either gradual or immediate, in the District of Columbia.   The property of the whole country, and the seat of our national government, the divine pressed upon Mr. Calhoun, the desirableness of its being entirely unpolluted by the touch of slavery.   At first the argument seemed to be little heeded, but at length, upon the condition that the measure should be entirely a Southern one, come from the South, and receive its advocacy, Mr. Calhoun consented to prepare such a bill, and arranged with his friend to visit Washington, whenever he should inform him that the details of the measure had been prepared. Nor was the promise forgotten. In the winter following these interviews, Mr. Calhoun summoned his friend to the capitol, informing him of his readiness to proceed with the proposed measure. The divine immediately complied with the invitation. He went to Washington, saw Mr. Calhoun, at his request, solicited two prominent Northern politicians to give to the proposed measure their influence ; and was, as he supposed, on the very eve of success, when suddenly the distinguished Southerner refused to take another step in the matter, alleging as his reason the violent anti-slavery feeling, that was then just beginning to manifest itself in some portions of New England.*

But from this view of the opposition to slavery, that was once almost universal in this land, it is time that we should turn, to inquire, for a moment, into the causes of that strange and marvelous change of sentiment that has, on this subject, recently taken place. For whatever may, in our early history, have been public opinion on this great question, no one can doubt but that there are few now, at the South, at least, who condemn this institution. Among Southern statesmen we look in vain for the men, who, in their views of slavery, sympathize with Patrick Henry, Washington, Jefferson, Madison, or of any of the other fathers of our republic; and we know of no prominent divine at the South, who would *now* vote for such a deliverance upon this subject, as was the unanimous utterance of the General Assembly of the Presbyterian Church in 1818. Upon this great moral question, *millions of people* have, in thirty years, or a little more, radically changed their sentiments. In this age of progress in art, education, and religion, we have beheld the strange phenomenon of whole States, converted from the opponents of involuntary servitude, into its stoutest defenders. Toward the great idea of universal liberty and equality, the race at large has, for the last half century, been steadily advancing. In the old world these principles battling with oppression has, from many of its seats of power, hurled it into the dust. Even in Russia serfdom has been abolished. It is in enlightened and Christian America alone, that the moral tone of society seems, in this respect, to have been lowered, that the public conscience has deteriorated, and that men have gone back, in their ideas of human rights, to barbaric ages.

But how was this sad change effected? What were the influences most potent in producing it?

* The writer of this article is fully aware of the fact, that the public will be slow to believe such a statement as this. We are all justly incredulous with reference to any alleged fact, in the history of a public man, that is *new*, and in opposition to the generally received estimate of his opinions. It is proper, therefore, definitely to state the authority upon which the above statement is made. The facts were mentioned to the writer by the "distinguished divine" himself, in conversation some years since. They are, likewise, contained in a letter, written at his dictation, and dated ————, October 6th, 1862. In this letter permission is given to the author to publish these facts. He regrets that he has not the liberty of adding the name of the eminent divine.

By many the whole problem is supposed to be solved, by the simple fact of the intemperate, and, oftentimes, uncharitable discussion of this subject at the North.   From the opponents of slavery, the *whole South* became its friends, we are told, because men, who had no personal contact with, or interest in this institution, indeed, who lived hundreds of miles from it, violently condemned it; wrote unkindly and hastily about it; petitioned Congress either to abolish it, or to prevent its extension; sought to bring odium upon all who were in any way engaged in it; and finally endeavored even to excite to a bloody insurrection those who were in bondage.   Had these men attended to their own concerns, had the Northern press and pulpit been silent on this subject, or had their utterances been more kind and considerate, we are assured that we would never have witnessed that strange revolution of sentiment to which we have just referred.

But is this so?   Is this cause sufficient to produce such an effect ?   We say nothing in reply of the admitted fact that the men who thus spoke and wrote, constituted but a small minority of the whole people of the North—we willingly waive this important consideration—nor would we yet again, here express any opinion as to their conduct, whether it was in itself right or wrong, for its influence might in either case, be the same   We would rather accept the most exaggerated statement that on this subject can be made, and unite in the severest condemnation of such conduct, while we yet assert that, as a cause, it is altogether *inadequate* to the effect. What ! nine millions of people, radically changed in sentiment upon a great moral question, converted to the most obstinate defense of slavery, brought to the point of regarding that institution as divine, and a blessing to both of the parties between whom it subsists, because a number of men, as large as themselves, and certainly their peers in intelligence and piety, regarded it as wicked, said so, and were unceasing, and, we will add, unscrupulous, in their efforts to destroy it !   Can any candid man believe that such a thing is possible?   That the feelings of the South have been deeply wounded by what they regarded as the meddlesomeness of the North with their peculiar institution, that they have been chafed and irritated by it, that they have regarded themselves as maligned, and that this conviction of injured innocence has, in some cases, led them to defend what, in other circumstances, they would have condemned, we cheerfully admit.   The result of persecution, either real or supposed, is, perhaps, always to endear to men that for which they are persecuted, and to lead them to stand up more stoutly in its defense. But one entire section of a great country revolutionized in sentiment upon a moral question, led to believe that a domestic institution was *right* that previously they had regarded as wrong, because the other section condemned it, and labored and prayed for its abolition, is not the very idea preposterous !

Suppose the case to be reversed ; suppose the whole South to have arraigned itself, in the most violent opposition, to the manufacture and sale of intoxicating drinks at the North, can we conceive that *we* here would have all become the champions of this traffic, and boldly affirmed it to be morally right ? It is time that the idea we are considering should be exploded. It has dwelt long enough in the bosoms of good men, as a sufficient apology, for one of the most marvelous changes of sentiment that the world has ever witnessed. We must look further, and deeper, for the real cause of this sad effect.

In the case of a single individual, we are all aware of the influence, that is exerted upon the moral judgment, by a long continuance in any line of conduct, or mode of life, that is *once* felt to be either positively wrong, or of doubtful propriety. As men live in the practice of sin, they lose both the consciousness, and the belief of its sinfulness. Self conditions faith. The power that perceives a wicked act, partakes of the general injury that that act, when performed, inflicts on the soul. As character deteriorates, so does the standard by which we judge of it. A man's own moral state and life is very much the measure of his moral convictions. Let any one have his conscience so enlightened, as to perceive that a certain pursuit in which he is engaged is wrong, but, despite that, let him still continue in it, and in time he will be very prone, not only to lose all convictions of its wickedness, but really to marvel how he could have ever cherished, with regard to it, such an opinion. It is by this principle alone, that we can explain the fact, that those most apt in this world to justify themselves, and in conscious innocence to say, "we have no sin," are ordinarily the most depraved. They have gone on so far in sin that it has become a *"hidden thing" to them*. Their moral sense is paralyzed. "In the lowered temperature of the inward consciousness, they have reached that point, where the growing coldness, hardness, and selfishness of a man's nature can no longer be noted ; the mechanism by which moral variations are indicated, having become itself insensible and motionless."

The principle is applicable to the case before us, and in it may be found one potent cause for the effect which we have described. There was a time, in the history of this country, when the conscience of the South was so enlightened, as to see that slavery was a great moral evil. Her statesmen saw it, and did not hesitate to proclaim it. Her divines saw it, and did not draw back, in the deliverances of the church, from uniting with others in condemning it. But, alas, to these convictions, expressed in political speeches, and church deliverances, there was no corresponding action. Slavery, seen to be an evil, was not immediately abolished, nor were any plans devised by which it might ultimately be destroyed. On the contrary, the institution was retained. Southern society, instead of seeking to cast off this net-work of evil, or to loosen the coils in which it was inwrapping it, suffered it to remain, and every day to tighten its grasp. The difficulties in the way of the emancipation of the enslaved were so exaggerated, as to be regarded as forever insurmountable. The behests of conscience were destroyed. The monitions of the moral sense were disregarded. Men went on doing what they knew to be wrong. They wilfully continued in sin. And, from such conduct, is it any marvel that, in time, just such results followed as we have described? Refusing to do anything for the freedom of the enslaved, when conscious that *duty* demanded it, is it strange that that bondage should finally come itself to be regarded as right?

We are well aware of the seriousness of the charge that we thus bring against the South. In what we have said, we aver nothing less, on this point, than their demoralization. We affirm that they are now the defenders of African slavery, because of a paralysis of their conscience, produced by the long continuance of this institution, *after* its true character was known. But can any candid mind doubt that this position is true? Is it not a conclusion logically irresistible? Do we not see the same principle repeating itself in the moral judgment of individuals all around us? To work a radical change, in the opinion of a man, upon the moral character of any action, is there anything more efficient than its habitual performance, after his conscience has once been enlightened to know that it is wrong?

But other causes have conspired, with the one just mentioned, in producing this wonderful revolution of sentiment at the South, with regard to slavery. During our colonial history, and for the first few years of our existence as a separate nation, when, as we have seen, the anti-slavery feeling was so strong, we have already had occasion to refer to the fact, that the growth of cotton in this country was inconsiderable. A writer in the Penny Cyclopædia presents us with this brief summary of facts :—

"In 1786 the total imports of cotton to the British isles was somewhat less than 20,000,000 pounds, *no part of which was furnished by North America*. Our West India colonies supplied nearly one-third, about an equal quantity was brought from foreign colonies in the same quarter, 2,000,000 pounds came from Brazil, and 5,000,000 pounds from the Levant. In 1790 the importation amounted to 31,447.605 pounds, *none of which was supplied by the United States*. In 1795 the quantity was only 26,401,340 pounds. In this year a commercial treaty was made between the United States of North America and Great Britain, by one article of which, as it originally stood, the export was prohibited from the United States, in American vessels, of such articles as they had previously imported from the West Indies. Among these articles *cotton was included; Mr. Jay, the American negotiator, not being aware that cotton was then becoming an article of export from the United States*. In 1800 the imports had more than doubled, having reached 56.010,732 pounds. *This was the first year* (1800) *in which any considerable quantity was obtained from America*, the imports from that quarter were about 16,000,000 pounds."[*]

But it happened that about this time, several causes came into operation which, in their effect, greatly increased, both the demand for cotton abroad, and its cultivation in this country. It was now that the inventions of Hargreaves, Arkwright, Crompton, and others, in cotton-spinning, were made, enabling English artisans successfully to compete with the weavers of India; and that the steam engine, having undergone the improvements of Watt, was first applied on a large scale to manufacturing industry. It was, likewise, at this time, that Whitney invented his saw-gin, an invention which strikingly supplemented those of which we have just spoken, and without which we, as a people, could have done little toward supplying that increased demand for cotton which these inventions of English artisans, had produced. Before this, the only cotton grown in America which was available for the general purposes of commerce, was that which was known as the Sea-Island kind. But this variety grew only in a few favored localities, and the quantity produced could never of necessity be large. The difficulty of separating the seed from the wool, by any methods then in use,

---

[*] Article *Cotton.*

was so great in the other varieties of cotton that could be grown on this continent, as to render them of little value for the ordinary purposes of trade. But this difficulty the invention of Whitney so completely overcome, as at once to bring into general demand the whole American crop.* In a suit brought by Whitney, in Savannah, in 1807, to sustain the validity of his patent, Judge Johnson thus speaks of the importance of this invention, and of its influence upon the industrial interests of the South :—

"The whole interior of the Southern States was languishing, and its inhabitants emigrating for want of some object to engage their attention and employ their industry, when the invention of this machine at once opened views to them which set the whole country in active motion. From childhood to age it has presented to us a lucrative employment. Individuals who were depressed with poverty and sunk in idleness, have suddenly risen to wealth and respectability. Our debts have been paid off, our capitals have increased, and our lands trebled themselves in value."†

Moreover, it should here be remarked, that African slavery, to be economical and permanent, must be applied to the production of some commodity which, while it is greatly in demand, requires only crude labor. In the more difficult industrial arts it cannot be profitably and safely employed, the general awakening of the faculties, intellectual and moral, produced by such pursuits, inevitably disqualifying men for a servile condition. But cotton is a commodity which fulfills these conditions.

And of these combined influences, the result was precisely what we should have anticipated. The Slave States became cotton-growing States. That plant, which heretofore had been cultivated mainly in the gardens of the South, and whose growth, for the purposes of trade, had been limited to a narrow belt of land running along the coast of South Carolina, now whitened scores of acres far inland. It was exported to Europe. It came into successful competition with that which had been grown in other countries. By its superior quality and low price, it gradually commanded for itself almost the whole market. Europe began now to look to America for her supply of this great staple of trade, and its growth elsewhere began materially to decline.

Moreover, through this exportation, the South was enabled to

* See Cairnes' Slave Power, p. 106.
† American Journal of Science, vol. xxi.

command the industrial resources of all commercial nations. Without cultivating for herself any art, or engaging in any skilled labor —as indeed she could not with her slaves do—she was yet able, through an exchange with other countries, to secure the products of the highest manufacturing and mechanical skill. *Wealth*, too, was thus secured to the slaveholders of the South. The value of cotton exported from this country, in 1858, has been estimated at nearly one hundred and thirty-two millions of dollars,* and to this must be added the sum realized from sales at home.

And from the commencement of this process, near the opening of the present century, it has been steadily going on. The following table—prepared after consulting all the authorities within our reach, and containing the total production of raw cotton in every part of our globe, together with the whole amount of the crop grown in the United States, at intervals of ten years—will perhaps present this subject more forcibly than we could do in words. In its examination, we beg that our readers will observe how impressively it teaches us these two great facts: the astonishing rapidity with which this trade has grown at the South, and the almost complete monopoly of it which at last was attained:—

Years.	Amount grown in the United States.	Total production of raw cotton.
	lbs.	*lbs.*
1791.......................	2,000,000	490,000,000
1801.......................	48,000,000	520,000,000
1811.......................	80,000,000	555,000,000
1821.......................	180,000,000	630,000,000
1831.......................	385,000,000	820,000,000
1841.......................	740,000,000	980,000,000
1851.......................	1,036,000,000	1,242,000,000

And now these facts, have they no connection with that great revolution of sentiment, with regard to the moral character of slavery, that has taken place at the South? Can any man think of them *together*, and believe that they are in *no way related?* When a business becomes highly profitable, is anything more common among men than the conviction of its rightfulness? A self-interested casuistry, is it not very prone to call in unsound pleas, and reasons, and excuses which, constantly pressing the line that

* New American Cyclopædia, article *Cotton*.

divides right from wrong, at last wholly removes it? In asserting this, we do nothing more than attribute to the South the foibles of our common humanity. The spectacle of either an individual, or a nation *condemning* that which enriches them, is very rare in this world of sin. Lord Bacon says: "I cannot call riches better than the baggage of virtue—the Roman word is better, 'impedimenta'—for, as the baggage is to an army, so is riches to virtue, * * it hindereth the march; * * yea, it sometimes loseth or disturbeth the victory."*

What a sad illustration of this truth do we discover in the history of this nation! With no great staple of trade that could be profitably cultivated by slave labor, and that was rapidly enriching the South, the institution of American slavery was almost universally condemned! With such a commodity, and in the possession of the monopoly of it, slavery is believed to be right; and, for its preservation and extension, it is thought to be no crime to deluge our country with blood, destroy our nationality, and extinguish to the world the last hope of free government.

---

* Lord Bacon's Works, vol. i. p. 42.

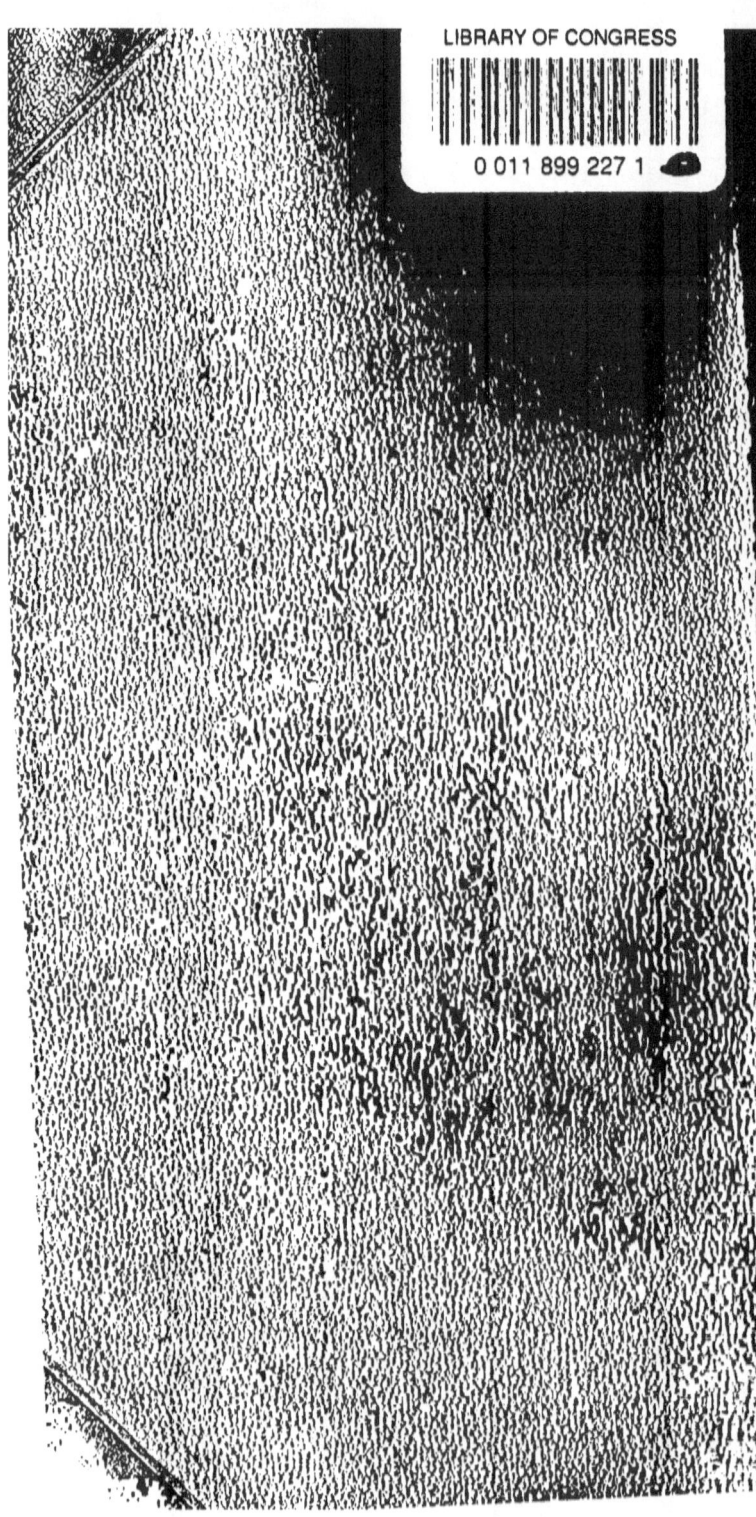